Let's talk about your leadership.

Learning through the art of storytelling

Written by Trish Kerin

Illustrated by Louise Kerin

Copyright © 2020 Trish Kerin

All rights reserved.

ISBN: 9798620483532

Contents

Acknowledgements i

Prologue 1

Chapter 1 Basis of leadership 3

Chapter 2 Key traits and actions – how they relate 5

Chapter 3 Be yourself 11

Chapter 4 Be consistent 12

Chapter 5 Seek out information and learn from others 13

Chapter 6 Set direction 14

Chapter 7 Speak up 15

Chapter 8 Reflect 16

Chapter 9 Look after people 17

Chapter 10 Have fun 18

Chapter 11 Wrap up 19

Acknowledgements

There are a few people I would like to acknowledge for their support and encouragement of me and my leadership development. Chris Chittenden, from Talking About, for being my leadership coach over the past 20 plus years. He has challenged me to be the best version of myself.

Majella Beagley, my amazing sister, for challenging my words and helping me improve them.

Louise Kerin, my talented niece, for providing the illustrations for this book. You can check out her work on Instagram @lkerin

And lastly, my biggest fan for their ongoing support and encouragement.

Prologue

I started my career as an engineering graduate who thought they knew it all, as most of us did. Very quickly I came to realise that I pretty much knew how to solve a problem and that was about all. From that day on I started my leadership journey, first by realising that I knew nothing.

I started work in an engineering department designing and constructing pipelines under tight schedules and then decided I wanted a change. I went to work in a refinery, on shift, working with operators who had so much more life experience and knowledge than I had. I learnt so much from those operators, how to work with people, motivate them, listen to them and, respect their experience. I made mistakes, many of them in fact, but I kept trying again. These lessons created a resilience and a trust in my capability, I just needed to be open to criticism and learning.

Over the years I progressed though different roles, which gave me a chance to continually improve my skills and become aware of my weaknesses. After many years of being a leader without any positional authority, I became a formal leader, with people responsibilities and accountabilities. The years of having only the ability of influence prepared me well for having authority, I realised I could not rely on my authority if I wanted to get the best out of my people, I needed to influence them – they needed to make the choices for themselves.

Before moving to my current role, I was privileged to be put in a leadership position to lead a culture change in an organisation. It was one of the most challenging roles I have ever done, but also one of the most rewarding. To see people develop and shine, choose their own destiny and achieve their goals was fantastic.

My role now is one of influence and not authority, but I have a chance to exercise that influence over multiple industry sectors around the world to advance process safety so everyone can go home from work at the end of their shift. I use all of the experiences and skills I have accumulated over my career to help me achieve my goals.

In this short poetry book, I will introduce you to the traits I believe are critical for a leader, and how these traits can be displayed in actions. It does not matter whether you are the Chief Executive Officer, or working on the front line, we all have a role to play and can all be a leader to someone.

I was once told that if I lowered my expectation of leadership I would not be so disappointed. But this is not the answer, we should not settle for poor leaders, we all need to be better, we should be able to have reasonable expectations of leaders, and not be disappointed.

I invite you to think about the best and worst leaders you have experienced, what made you feel good and perform at your best? What made you feel bad, resulting in underperformance? How can you use some of those lessons and the ones contained in this book to take your leadership to the next level and amplify your team's performance?

Chapter 1 Basis of leadership

There are many different definitions of what leadership is. Some conflict with each other, some compliment each other and there are many research based books you can read. This book summarises leadership at its most basic premise, and is based on my experience of what worked for me.

Leadership is all about people, other people, the people you lead, it is not about you. If you can support your people to help them be the best that they can be, and help them achieve their goals and aims. This, to me, is what leadership is about.

When a team is performing well, people see the team, when a team is performing badly, people see the leader. In this way, a leader needs to be selfless, when the team does well, it reflects well on everyone, including the leader, but they are not on a pedestal. The leader should not receive the accolades personally, these need to be shared among the team. Ultimately the leaders must be accountable for the team's performance, so when the team fails, the leader is often blamed. We see this most prevalently in sporting teams. When the team wins the highest prize, it was the team, when the team finishes last, the coach is often blamed, and removed. This sounds harsh, after all the coach was not on the field, they did not miss the goal, but it is their role to motivate and upskill the team to work together to be their best. This means that leadership is an act of sacrifice and service, and this can sometimes be the most difficult part to accept.

Being a leader also often requires tough conversations when things are not going well. Sometimes this means we need to reprimand people in the team. This is necessary to ensure everyone knows the requirements and boundaries, but it must always be done justly and with respect.

There are some specific traits that I believe all leaders should have and these are then demonstrated by actions. These are covered in the next chapter.

Chapter 2 Key traits and actions – how they relate

Over my career I have observed some exceptional leaders and some leaders who I judged to be poor. This has led me to develop a list of the key traits I saw in the exceptional leaders. I do not think leaders are only born, I think they can be made with effort and practice.

Here are my key traits for every leader.

Be **inspirational**

People look to a leader for guidance and inspiration, so you need to be inspirational. But this does not mean you need to be charismatic. Charisma is different to inspiration, though sometimes it can be difficult to recognise the difference, because charisma tends to be omnipresent – we see it straight away. But underneath, charisma lacks substance, and this is where inspiration comes to the fore. Inspiration comes from having passion for what you do. Passion is contagious with people, they want to be part of it, and this inspires them to join. I have worked with leaders who I would never describe as charismatic, but they were inspirational.

Have **vision**

You cannot lead people if you don't know where you are going, they will not stay for a journey with no vision. So you need to have a path through out, and communicate this path to the team. When they understand the vision, you can even lead them from behind or within, being there for support, but they know the way, so they can keep journeying.

Be **trustworthy**

When you ask a person to do something, they need to trust that you have their interests at heart. This means you need to build trust with them. To build trust your actions must match your words. You also need to work within your competence and be capable.[1] A track record of delivering on your promises is important. These elements will show that you are of a trustworthy character. When times are tough, your team needs to trust you to come through.

Serve others

We often forget that leadership is an act of service, the leader is there to serve the needs of the team, not the other way around. By helping the team members, removing roadblocks for them and supporting them, they will be able to perform at their best. If they are constantly busy serving the needs of the leader, rather than fulfilling their role, they will not achieve the outcomes that are sought. This is often one of the most difficult aspects, it is so tempting to get the team to do your work, but your role is to make their work easier to accomplish. This is not to say that you are at their mercy, but neither are they at yours.

Be **empathetic**

If you cannot put yourself in the shoes of another, you cannot support them effectively through a difficult time. Being empathetic is different to being sympathetic. They do not need your sympathy, you do not need to feel for them, but you need to understand how they are feeling. Are they stressed because of job uncertainty? Unless you realise this, you will not be able to work with them to get them focused to get the job done effectively.

Be **humble**

Being humble goes hand in hand with serving others. You must recognise that you are not better or worse than anyone else. If you think as the leader you are superior to the team, you will trip up sooner or later. It is about thinking more about the needs of the team

---

[1] adapted from Talking About Pty. Ltd © 2004-2011

and the outcome, instead of thinking about yourself more. This can sometimes be tied up in a person's ego, and whether they feel accomplishment in their team's successes or only in their own successes. People are also less intimidated by a humble person. This does not mean that you may not have a commanding presence, but it will be a presence that people want to be part of, not fear.

It is easy to talk about traits, but how can they be related to actions, and what would those actions look like? I have eight actions which epitomise the traits discussed in this book. These are detailed here, including what traits they align to.

Be yourself – be trustworthy

In general people seem to be a good judge of character, they can identify if we are being disingenuous. This will create a level of distrust. While we are often tempted to emulate leaders who we are inspired by, we cannot do this at the expense of being ourselves. This does not mean we should put all our worst traits on display for everyone to see, it is not an excuse to be rude or difficult. However, you can hone your best skills and display them, be yourself with skill! We are all unique and should value that, as we can all contribute something different and add to the outcomes. Remember sometimes slipping into a negative trait is human and shows vulnerability – which can be positive for building relationships and trust, because it makes you relatable.

Be consistent – be trustworthy

It is very difficult working for someone who is unpredictable. As humans we like to know what to expect in most situations, and this is why consistency from a leader is critical. Being consistent also goes a long way to building trust, because your actions match your words. It is important to clearly set expectations for people, and these too need to be consistent.

Seek out information and learn from others – be humble

We sometimes think that leaders need to have all the answers. This is not true; they just need to know where to go to find the answers.

This means you need to be willing to ask questions and listen to the answers. If you are not going to genuinely listen to the answer, you are better off not asking the question, because ignoring the answer does more damage to your reputation than not asking the question. The person may think you don't care if you don't ask, but if you ignore the answer you have proven you don't care. This does not mean you need to agree with the answer, but you cannot ignore it. As a leader, ignorance is not excuse, you are expected to have sought the answer, not doing so in negligent. We also need to be willing to admit that we don't know the answer sometimes, but we can commit to finding it. This willingness to admit you don't know something shows humility.

Set direction – be inspirational, have vision

Follow the leader! This means the leader has to know where they are going, otherwise you may as well be following them into oblivion. So, it is critical for a leader to set the direction, but they also need to share that direction with the team, so that the team can continue along the path, when the leader may not be available. This requires the leader to have a vision of what the future can look like, and to then inspire people to believe in the vision. They will then want to go on the journey to get there. It seems cliché to talk about the journey, but simply put, leadership is all about the journey. As I said earlier, to be inspirational, you do not need to be charismatic, but you need to be able to communicate your vision, and if this is done with genuine passion, it will be inspiring.

Speak up – serve others, be empathetic

We all need to have the courage to speak up when we see something is not right. If we simply ignore the issue, we are in fact condoning it, because our actions speak louder than our lack of words. It can be difficult to speak up, because sometimes what we need to say may not be popular, or it may create some issues, but we need to be courageous to serve our teams. Afterall, as the leader we cannot expect our teams to speak up when something is wrong, if we have never shown the courage to do it ourselves. To help our teams speak up, we also need to give them permission to do so. Give them permission to give us feedback, make suggestions or challenge our decisions. I have always allowed my teams to challenge my decisions, it is one of the first ground rules I set. We can then have a discussion, and sometimes they convince me to change my decisions, sometimes my decision stands, but the conversation that leads to that point is vital in the effective functioning of the team.

Reflect – be humble

Our lives are so busy now, that we often don't make time to quietly reflect on what is happening. Reflection can be about understanding what we did and how we could have done it better. This is our opportunity to learn for the next time. It can also be about understanding how we did well and thinking about how to apply that to the next situation to improve outcomes. It is also important to make sure that you celebrate success, we are always quick to focus on failure, but less often celebrate what went well in the workplace. This can be done by once a week having the team email their successes to everyone else. It can build a sense of celebrating each other's successes and supporting the team. I learnt this from someone who worked with me. Celebrating a success can be inspiring for people. It need not be something material, and is often better to have no monetary value, but it must be genuine. But looking at oneself requires humility, because we won't always like what we see, but we need the maturity to learn from it.

Look after people – serve others, be empathetic

If you do not take care of your people, they will take care of themselves, usually by leaving. Your role as a leader is to nurture and develop the team so they can perform at their best. You do not need to have a team full of superstars to have a superstar performing team, you just need to support everyone to be the best they can be. This means you need to understand what they are feeling and what motivates them, because each person is motivated differently. A one size fits all approach rarely works. This means you need to get to know them and understand their situations. They might be distracted by something happening in their lives, so how can you support them to get the best performance in the circumstances.

Have fun– serve others, be empathetic

In the same way that we often don't make time to reflect, we often don't make time to have fun at work. Afterall it's called work, not fun! But sometimes some light heartedness can ease tension and allow people to think more clearly. We know that feeling when there is a big issue that we are stuck on, everyone is stressed, and someone cracks a joke. The tension dissipates and we can then see the path forward. Rather then relying on someone to crack the joke, we can plan to have fun. Maybe you have a team coffee break once a week and set a theme for people to participate in. It can be helpful to think of work as a game. You need to know what the rules are so you can play the game and you need to understand the stakes. Sometimes the stakes may be high, if it goes wrong, people can die, other times the stakes may be low, you might lose a small amount of money. The stakes can change the rules of the game, but you can adapt the rules yourself.

So I have laid out my basis of leadership as well as my key traits and actions. The next 9 chapters are fun poems based on the actions, using the art of storytelling to convey learning in a more memorable way. We often forget this art as we grow older. As children we learn many life lessons from stories, and as we age we forget the importance of stories. They become "childish" to us, but they can be very effective in communicating and teaching a lesson. Sometimes we need to remember that stories are an effective communication tool, not a childish indulgence. Please enjoy the poems and take on board the learnings – it may just make you a better leader.

So now onto the fun.

Chapter 3 Be yourself

Let's talk about your lea-der-ship,

With others work in fellowship.

We are all in-di-vid-u-als,

We all have our own prin-ci-ples.

Trying to be someone else?

It's best to always be yourself!

Everyone's skills are all unique,

That is what we bring, so to speak!

To all these actions you must cling,

You really have so much to bring!

Chapter 4 Be consistent

Let's talk about your lea-der-ship,

Con-sis-ten-cy's the internship.

We all must set the goal posts clear,

Or it will confuse you, I fear!

The rules consistent for us all,

No cla-ri-ty? We go AWOL!

Ad-her-ence is in-te-gral,

Making our lives pre-dict-able!

To all these actions you must cling,

You really have so much to bring!

Chapter 5 Seek out information and learn from others

Let's talk about your lea-der-ship,

Leading is not an ego trip!

When making several su-gges-tions,

Always keep in mind the questions.

It's in-for-ma-tion you require,

Of all facts you must enquire.

Even though you sometimes stumble,

Re-mem-ber, always be humble.

To all these actions you must cling,

You really have so much to bring!

Chapter 6 Set direction

Let's talk about your lea-der-ship,

It's important to steer the ship.

You may not be the CEO,

But we need to know where to go!

We should think about the out-come,

For barriers, we'll over-come.

Let's set the pathway to-ge-ther,

Diff-i-cul-ties we will wea-ther.

To all these actions you must cling,

You really have so much to bring!

Chapter 7 Speak up

Let's talk about your lea-der-ship,

Let us not sched-ule a guilt trip.

Al-ways make sure your voice is heard,

It's so ea-sy to miss a word.

When things are wrong you must speak up,

It's not a storm in a tea-cup!

They may not like what you must say,

But say it you must, anyway!

To all these actions you must cling,

You really have so much to bring!

Chapter 8 Reflect

Let's talk about your lea-der-ship,

Time to ponder your ow-ner-ship.

Don't get caught up in all the noise,

Remember always keep your poise.

A mirror used to help you see,

To be the best that you can be.

Some failure may cause you distress,

But stop! Celebrate the success!

To all these actions you must cling,

You really have so much to bring!

Chapter 9 Look after people

Let's talk about your lea-der-ship,

It's not about brink-man-ship.

Steer clear of all the po-li-tics,

Trust can deal with all the scep-tics.

People need constant nur-tur-ing,

A-ssist in talent sur-fa-cing.

You must always be fair and just,

Otherwise there will be mistrust.

To all these actions you must cling,

You really have so much to bring!

Chapter 10 Have fun

Let's talk about your lea-der-ship,

Let's start your fun ap-pren-tice-ship.

Remember work is just a game,

Though all the stakes are not the same.

When it is time to have a laugh,

Joking around may help the staff.

Light-heartedness relieves the stress,

Helping us deal with all the mess.

To all these actions you must cling,

You really have so much to bring!

Chapter 11 Wrap up

So now we have explored each action, let's look at them all together. The poem below focuses on applying leadership to safety, but you can apply it to many situations.

Do you like this safety thing?

Do you like this safety thing?

Or are you not sure what to bring?

Let's talk about your leadership,

On what do you have a grip?

It's all important to be yourself,

And consistency is just top shelf!

Of information, you must seek,

Learn from others stickybeak!

You must decide which way to go,

Sometimes you'll host a speaking show.

Always make time for your reflecting,

And remember, people need protecting!

Your workload may be big to run,

But never forget to have some fun!

Do you like this safety thing?

I do! I have so much to bring!

www.ingramcontent.com/pod-product-compliance
Lightning Source LLC
Chambersburg PA
CBHW040056250526
45473CB00042B/2849